All About the
Appalachian Trail

Leonard M. Adkins

BLUE
RIVER
PRESS

All About the Appalachian Trail
Copyright © 2020 by Leonard M. Adkins

Published by Blue River Press
Indianapolis, Indiana
www.brpressbooks.com

Distributed by Cardinal Publishers Group
A Tom Doherty Company, Inc.
www.cardinalpub.com

ISBN: 978-1-68157-099-0

Cover Design: David Miles
Cover Artist: Robert Perrish
Book Design: Dave Reed
Illustrator: Kirsten Halvorsen
Editor: Dani McCormick
Special Thanks to the Appalachian Trail Museum

Printed in the United States of America

10 9 8 7 6 5 4 3 2 1   20 21 22 23 24 25 26 27

Contents

All About the Appalachian Trail

Preface

The Appalachian Trail is a footpath located in the eastern United States. It is close to 2,200 miles long. The pathway crosses many roads. This makes it possible for people to choose to do very long or short hikes. In addition, it goes into or near a number of small towns.

The trail also passes through eight national forests, numerous state parks, and six national parks. One national park is the Great Smoky Mountains National Park in Tennessee and North Carolina. Another is Shenandoah National Park in Virginia.

The Appalachian Trail was completed in 1937. In 1968 it was designated the first National Scenic Trail. After that, the pathway became a part of the national park system.

The Appalachian Trail is simply called the "AT" by those who hike on it. The pathway goes through 14 states on its way from Georgia to

Maine. It follows the route of the Appalachian Mountains. Because of this, it is not a flat trail. It goes up and down a lot. Hiking the entire trail would be like climbing Mount Everest, the world's tallest mountain, 16 times.

The AT touches upon nearly every environment to be found in the Appalachian Mountains. Sometimes there are wide views from lofty ridgelines. There are quiet, hidden campsites in narrow valleys. Miles of trail go through tunnels of rhododendron bushes. There is also the chance to see big animals like bears and moose. Small creatures such as frogs and salamanders live there, too.

The trail is not just a walk through nature. It also is an introduction to America's history. It goes by Civil War locations and a village where freed slaves lived. There are old water mill sites and places where American Indian tribes battled. The AT also provides a look at modern America by going into small towns.

Close to three million people a year visit the Appalachian Trail. Some take just a few steps from their car to enjoy a nearby view. Many come to hike for a few hours and to get exercise outdoors. Others, like Scout troops or families, hike for a day or two. They will sleep in a tent in the woods at night.

There are also people who try to walk the entire trail in one long hike. They are called "thru-hikers" and it will take them from four to six months. If they are successful, the Appalachian Trail Conservancy awards them a certificate. It officially declares that the person has reached their goal. He or she is then known as a "2,000 Miler."

It is not just people from America who walk this pathway. It has become famous throughout the world. Men, women, and children come from many other countries. Some have been from Canada, Germany, Israel, Thailand, Palestine, France, South Africa, England, and Austria.

Volunteers do most of the work on the Appalachian Trail. More than 6,500 people volunteer each year. They work more than 250,000 hours to build, maintain, and protect the pathway. It is a place where your family and friends can hike and enjoy the outdoors.

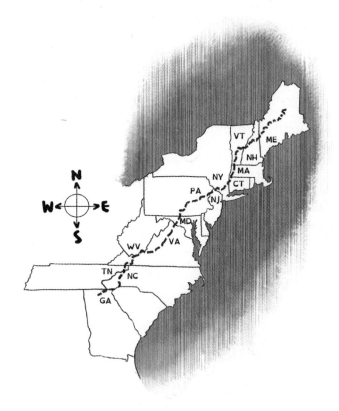

From south to north, the Appalachian Trail goes through: Georgia, North Carolina, Tennessee, Virginia, West Virginia, Virginia again, Maryland, Pennsylvania, New Jersey, New York, Connecticut, Massachusetts, Vermont, New Hampshire, and Maine.

Chapter 1
How the
Mountains Formed

The Appalachian Mountains, like other mountain ranges, have gone through many changes in their history. The land has been subjected to the movements of Earth's crustal plates. Each time the plates collided, North America took on a new look. These giant land masses would grind into each other. This caused the Earth's surface to fold upward, creating mountains.

You can demonstrate the process in just a few seconds. Put a throw rug flat on a floor. Then push on one side while someone holds the other side in place. The rug will wrinkle and fold just like the Earth's surface.

About 270 million years ago, the continents that would become North America and Africa collided. This happened over the course of many millions of years. The land was pushed upward and the huge pile of rocks became the Appalachian Mountains.

Changes also started to take place in the animal and plant worlds. Insects began to fly and some aquatic life left their watery homes to become land animals. Giant ferns and clubmosses covered the continent. For millions of years they grew, died, and decomposed. Layer upon layer then compressed into the coal we use today.

About 200 million years ago the forces that created the Appalachians Mountains ended. The continents slowly began to separate. However, the mountains then did not look like the mountains upon which we hike. They were probably as high as Colorado's Rocky Mountains or South America's Andes are today. It was glaciers and erosion that shaped them into what we see today.

Earth has experienced dozens of different glacial episodes throughout its history. The last ended about 10,000 years ago. Advancing from the north, sheets of ice slid their way through the northern Appalachian Mountains. The glaciers eventually halted their movement in what is now called Pennsylvania. The ice sheets were so thick that they covered the summits of most mountains.

As they moved southward, the glaciers made dramatic changes in the landscape. Hike in New Hampshire's White Mountains and you can observe these changes first hand. The glaciers forced their way through once narrow river gorges. This scoured the hillsides and turned them into the U-shaped valleys seen today.

Glaciers carved the smooth sides of Mount Katahdin in Maine.

Sometimes on the higher ridgelines, the ice scraped off soil and vegetation. This left a smooth appearance on the rock. The even-surfaced stone on New York's Bear Mountain is evidence glaciers passed over it.

Trees and other plants helped crack
the stone gradually causing the mountain to erode.

Glaciers also scraped out large holes that filled with water once the ice melted. New Jersey's Sunfish Pond is the southern-most glacial pond on the Appalachian Trail. Massachusetts's Gore

Pond and Vermont's Griffith Lake are two of the more scenic and well-known.

However, erosion is the major force that changed the mountains. Both mechanical and chemical actions come into play during the erosion process.

Have you seen how tiny clumps of grass can crack a sidewalk? In the same way, tree and shrub roots break apart large rocks. Windblown particles also eat away at surface rocks like sandpaper. The smaller pieces then become subject to other types of weathering.

Water has the largest role in the process of erosion. Water seeps into cracks of rock and expands as it freezes. It then breaks the rock like the roots of plants do. Rain waters wash over these smaller pieces. This causes them to erode even more and become smaller and wash into creeks. These small streams then carry away the small pieces of the mountains.

Chemical processes also come into play. Some minerals dissolve in water and are carried away downstream. Rain water also has some acid in it. This can dissolve elements in the rocks. The rocks crumble and break, like rust damages the metal body of a car.

Lichens are small plants that grow on rocks. They erode rock both mechanically and chemically. The lichen's roots pry loose small bits of the rock. Also, a weak acid in the lichen chemically dissolves the rock's minerals, hastening additional wear.

So, what happens to all of this rock that is being broken and dissolved? Moved by rain and rivers, it may travel far from the mountains. Some may be deposited in the rich soil of the Piedmont. Others may help make up the clay on the Coastal Plain. Finally, some may even be carried all of the way out to sea.

This means beach sand may have come from the mountains. Think about the sand used to build a castle on Virginia Beach. It may have once been on a mountain along the Appalachian Trail.

Chapter 2
History of the Appalachian Trail

Benton MacKaye is known as the father of the Appalachian Trail.

In 1921, Benton MacKaye, whose last name rhymes with sky, proposed a very long hiking trail.

It would be built in the Appalachian Mountains of the eastern United States.

One year later, some people built the first miles of the Appalachian Trail. This was in state parks in New York. People in other states also began to work to see the dream become a reality. The Appalachian Trail Conference (now called the Appalachian Trail Conservancy or ATC) was formed in 1925. It was created to help coordinate all of those efforts.

Arthur Perkins enlisted many volunteers to help build the Appalachian Trail.

In 1928, retired Connecticut judge Arthur Perkins was appointed ATC chairman. He had taken over his family law firm, Perkins & Perkins, from his father after graduating from Yale. A lifetime lover of the outdoors, he also joined the Appalachian Mountain Club. Perkins brought another important man to the AT, Myron Avery.

Benton MacKaye was the vocal advocate of the Appalachian Trail. However, he did very little, if any, building of the trail. It is Myron Avery who is often credited with making the trail a reality. He was ATC chairman from 1931 to 1952. He worked on the trail nearly every weekend throughout those years. Sometimes he scouted the route of the pathway or helped other people build the trail. Other times he measured a newly constructed section of the pathway. By doing so, he became the first person to walk its full length.

Myron Avery also spread the word about the AT and recruited hundreds of volunteers.

First they had to go to the woods to decide where the trail would be located. Then they had to get the owner's permission to put the trail

Myron Avery used a bicycle wheel with a handle on it to measure the length of the trail.

there. Sometimes it was routed on private land. Other times the trail could go through public lands. This included national and state parks.

Once volunteers had permission they could begin building the trail. They had to carry picks, shovels, and saws many miles uphill. Sometimes the work involved moving 1,000 pound boulders. Sometimes they had to dig out automobile-sized root balls. They had to clear away entangling thorn bushes and poison ivy vines. Hand saws were used to cut tree trunks and limbs.

In 1948, Earl V. Shaffer became the first person to hike the entire AT in one journey.

It took a lot of hard work. So, it is remarkable that the trail was completed in just 16 years in 1937. Most of the physical labor was done by volunteers. They were not paid to do the work. They did so willingly because of their love of the outdoors. They also knew they were contributing to the completion of a noble project.

Just one year after the trail was completed, there was a major hurricane. It killed 700 people and left 60,000 homeless. It also destroyed so many miles of trail that volunteers were overwhelmed. Then construction of the Blue Ridge Parkway displaced 100 miles of the AT. More miles fell into disrepair during World War II. People began to wonder if the AT would ever again be one continuous route.

Things were looking bleak for the trail. Soon, however, popular heroes appeared. Their exploits inspired people to take action.

Earl V. Shaffer, who lived in Pennsylvania, set out to hike the AT in April, 1948. He started hiking at Mount Oglethorpe, the southern end of the AT at the time. He completed

Mildred Ryder depended on the kindness of strangers for food and shelter during her walk for peace.

the trail atop Mount Katahdin in Maine on August 5. It was such an amazing accomplishment that people did not believe him. However, he kept a very detailed journal and took many pictures. This convinced those who doubted, and he became known as the trail's first thru-hiker.

Three years later, Gene Espey duplicated the feat. One year after that, Mildred Ryder became the first woman thru-hiker. She gained the courage from her trek to embark upon a mission. In 1953, she started a journey that lasted 28 years. She walked more than 25,000 miles for peace. She became known as the Peace Pilgrim.

In 1955, Emma "Grandma" Gatewood became the first woman to thru-hike the trail alone. She was 67 years old. Her gear was carried in a duffel bag over her shoulders. Her shoes

An 'A' with a 'T' in the middle of it has become the symbol for the Appalachian Trail.

were sneakers. She eventually became the first person to hike the entire AT three times.

The exploits of these people revived interest in the trail. Then volunteers began to do more than just work on the pathway.

Mining, timbering, housing projects, new roadways, and more were intruding on the trail. These things detracted from its wilderness experience. In response, trail supporters got the National Trails System Act passed in 1968. It named the AT and the Pacific Crest Trail the country's first two national scenic trails. It also provided a small amount of money to buy land.

Further volunteer efforts resulted in the 1978 amendments to the National Trails System Act. It gave additional money to purchase land. This has been very successful. At the time of the act, less than 1,250 miles of the trail were on public lands. Today less than three miles remain to be brought under public protection.

It must be acknowledged that some of the private land was not sold willingly. But the many benefits cannot be denied. Millions of AT visitors have enjoyed these forested lands. They might have become housing developments or resorts if still in private hands.

Today, about 30 local trail clubs maintain the AT. Their volunteers continue the work that the first volunteers did. They still need to clear brush and weeds away from the trail. New blazes have to be painted on trees so hikers know where the trail goes. Shelters may need new roofs put on them. Fallen trees have to be sawed into small pieces and carried away.

These trail clubs welcome anyone that wants to help them maintain the trail. Children are welcome, too. If they can't do the very hard work, they can pull up weeds. Or carry away small branches or dig small rocks out of the ground. Sometimes they are even permitted to paint some of the blazes. Volunteers who devote numerous hours to working on the trail are given rewards by some clubs. These rewards may be patches, water bottles, hats, or t-shirts.

The local clubs also sponsor hikes on the trail. The outings are usually open to anyone who would like to go along.

In 1984, the National Park Service made volunteers officially responsible for maintaining the trail. This was historic. It was the first time ever that private citizens were entrusted to care for public lands.

Sometimes those efforts don't come in the form of physically working on the trail. Sometimes volunteers must respond to threats that would destroy the integrity of the trail. One of those times took place in Virginia. In 1996 there were plans to build a four-lane highway across the AT. This would cut the Mount Rogers National Recreation Area in half. It would have also turned Comers Creek Falls into a concrete culvert. The government cancelled the road after receiving hundreds of letters in protest.

The AT is a good example of how one person's idea can make a difference. It was only one man, Benton MacKaye, who dreamed of the Appalachian Trail. Yet, it was just this one man's idea that has inspired many others. Millions are now able to enjoy the beauty of nature while getting exercise. You can, too. Just by taking a simple walk in the woods.

Chapter 3

Southern States

Springer Mountain, Georgia, is the southern end of the Appalachian Trail today. It is 70 miles north of Atlanta. A plaque says, "APPALACHIAN TRAIL, GEORGIA TO MAINE: A Foothpath for those who seek Friendship with the Wilderness." There is also a good view of the mountains.

The start of the Appalachian Trail was moved from Mount Oglethorpe to Springer Mountain in 1958.

For the first half of the AT, the trail is in the Blue Ridge Mountains. It is then located on numerous other mountain ranges. Some of them are called the Poconos, Great Smoky, White, Green, and Mahoosuc Mountains. Yet, all of them are part of the Appalachian Mountain range. This can be confusing. Just think about the city you live in. It is part of a county, which is also part of a state. All of these are separate, but they are all a part of America.

The side trail that leads to the fifty-foot-tall Long Creek Falls is only about one-tenth of a mile long and is surrounded by beautiful wild rhododendron bushes.

From Springer Mountain, the AT goes northward. It goes next to Long Creek Falls. There are many waterfalls along the Appalachian

Trail. Long Creek Falls is one of the prettiest. It is surrounded by rhododendron bushes.

The AT then rises above 4,000 feet for the first time on Blood Mountain. A legend says the Cherokee and Creek tribes fought here hundreds of years ago. The battle was so fierce that the mountain was covered in blood.

Blood Mountain is a popular destination for hikers. There is a wide view of the Blue Ridge Mountains in all directions. On very clear days it

The Walasi-yi Interpretive Center
is the first mail-drop available to northbound hikers
that doesn't make them leave the trail.

is possible to see southward to Springer Mountain and beyond to Atlanta 85 miles away.

In Neels Gap, the AT passes through a place called Mountain Crossings at Walasi-Yi. This is the only building that the trail ever goes through.

In Chattahoochee Gap, the AT goes by a small spring that is the start of the Chattahoochee River. This river supplies drinking water for millions of people. It flows out of the mountains and goes through Atlanta. It eventually ends up at the Gulf of Mexico.

Once in North Carolina, the AT stays above 4,000 feet in elevation for 26 miles. The trail then steeply drops nearly 3,000 feet to a river. Many people come here to take whitewater rafting trips. This gorge is so deep and narrow that the Cherokee called it Nantahala. The word means "Land-of-the-Noon-Day-Sun."

Many different tribes of native people lived in eastern North America when European settlers arrived. The Cherokees were the only tribe to actually live upon the heights of the Appalachian mountain range.

Later, the United States government forced the Cherokees off their land. Part of the reason is European settlers wanted to live on that land. However, one of the main reasons is people wanted the gold that had been discovered there.

Driven by soldiers, 17,000 Cherokee were forced to march to Oklahoma in 1838. This became known as the "Trail of Tears." About 4,000 of the Cherokees died along the way. About 1,000 managed to escape into the mountains. After many years of hiding, they were permitted to establish the Qualla Reservation. Also called the Qualla Boundary, it's along the eastern edge of the Great Smoky Mountains.

America had a great desire for lumber in the late 1800s. By the 1920s many places were bare of trees. Plants help hold soil and prevent it from eroding with wind and water. Without the plants, the bare stone was exposed to the weather, which was destroying the mountains. In 1934, Great Smoky Mountains National Park was established, in part, to help the mountains heal.

Appalachian Trail visitors now hike through a very lush forest in the national park. Some people complain about the Appalachian Trail's few views. They call the pathway "The Long Green Tunnel."

These people are missing the true beauty of the Appalachian Mountains. Almost nowhere else in the world is there such a great variety of plants. In the Great Smoky Mountains alone there are more tree species than in all of Europe.

Of course, there are good views in the Great Smoky Mountains. One of the best is Clingmans Dome. A distinctive spiral walkway rises above the trees. It provides a 360-degree view of the mountains. This can be reached by hiking the AT. It can also be reached by a trail from a nearby parking lot. At 6,643 feet, Clingmans Dome is the highest point of the entire AT.

North of the Great Smoky Mountains, the AT goes over the Southern Bald Mountains. This is along the North Carolina/Tennessee border. Sometimes a hiker's right foot is in North Carolina at the same time the hiker's left foot is in Tennessee.

The visibility of Clingmans Dome Observation Tower is usually about 20 miles, but on clear days it reaches 100 miles.

These mountains have big grassy meadows on or near their summits. It is a mystery why because mountains nearby have trees on top. Some scientists think these meadows were grazed by prehistoric animals. Others believe the balds were created by native tribes. Whatever the reason, hikers like them because they offer far-ranging views.

Growing on the lower portions of these mountains are ramps. They are small wild onions

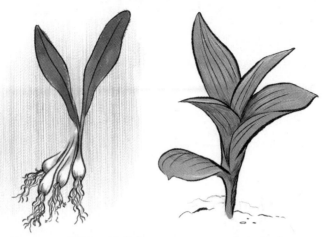

Ramps and False Hellebore are commonly mistaken for each other, but the easiest way to tell them apart is by smell. Ramps have a very strong odor.

that taste like garlic. Some people like to eat them. False hellebore also grows in the same area. It looks a little bit like a ramp when it first starts to grow. However, it is poisonous.

Another name for false hellebore is Indian Poke. This is because, according to legend, some American Indians would eat it. If they survived, they became a leader of their tribe. However, no one is sure if this is true or not.

A recent AT thru-hiker mistook a false hellebore for a ramp. He had a night of sweating, vomiting, and stomach cramps!

The AT goes by Watauga Lake just before entering Virginia. The lake is popular for fishing and boating. It was created in the 1940s by the Tennessee Valley Authority. The authority was started in the 1930s to help bring electricity to the southern United States and stop flooding.

Watauga Dam was finished in 1948. Unfortunately, the town of Butler was flooded after its construction and is now at the bottom of Watauga Lake.

Chapter 4
Virginia and West Virginia

There are more than 550 miles of the AT in Virginia. That is one-fourth of the entire length of the trail.

From the south, the trail comes into Virginia at the town of Damascus. This is one of the few towns that the trail actually passes through. Damascus calls itself "the friendliest town on the Appalachian Trail."

There are many services for AT visitors, including hostels. Hostels are lower-cost places where hikers can take showers and spend the night indoors. This is often in large rooms shared with other hikers in bunk beds. Although sometimes crowded, the hostels are usually happy places where hikers enjoy being with their friends. There are numerous hostels located close to the trail from Georgia to Maine.

Everyone, not just hikers, is invited to the town's Trail Days Festival every May. It is a fun way to meet hikers, learn about hiking and equipment, and join in a parade through town.

Another pathway, the Virginia Creeper Trail, goes through Damascus. Some people rent bikes and have a van drive them to the top of the mountain to ride back down. From there it is 18 miles back to Damascus. It is easy riding because it is almost all downhill. Very little peddling is needed.

From Damascus, the AT rises to the Mount Rogers National Recreation Area. This is a very

Wild ponies eat the vegetation
and help keep meadows from overgrowing.

popular place. That is because it has thousands of acres of open meadows. With such far-off vistas, the area reminds people of the Continental Divide in Montana and Wyoming. Herds of grazing wild ponies add to the feeling of being in the American West.

The ponies are small and their manes are long. Some of the manes are blond, others are black. Some of the ponies are brown. Some ponies are spotted. These small horses are comfortable with humans and will sometimes come close. This can be exciting, but they are wild animals and should not be fed. Just take some photographs so that you can enjoy this memory later.

Near Roanoke, the AT goes by what thru-hiker Laurie Messick called the "Triple Crown of Views." One place is called Dragon's Tooth. It was named this because it is a rock formation that juts out of the ground. This reminded people of how teeth on a dragon's lower jaw might have looked. People who make this rugged hike are rewarded with a nice view. Some even climb onto the tooth.

Dragon's tooth is a monolith of Tuscarora quartzite at the top of Cove Mountain near the McAfee Knob.

Many hikers believe McAfee Knob has the best view from the AT in Virginia. It is a large rock that juts out into space. In fact, the Appalachian Trail Conservancy says this is the most photographed scene on the trail. Some people have their picture taken while being near the edge. The knob is reached by a hike of almost four miles from a parking lot. From the knob, it's possible to see 80 miles of where the trail goes.

The AT follows the sheer rock wall of Tinker Cliffs for about a half mile. It, too, provides very nice views. Those include looks back to McAfee Knob and Dragon's Tooth.

The AT then goes close to the Blue Ridge Parkway for more than 100 miles. The parkway is a scenic highway more than 400 miles long. It is in Virginia and North Carolina. This is one

The rock that juts out into space on McAfee Knob is known as 'The Anvil.'

of the most visited parts of America's national park system. In addition to the AT, the parkway has many other trails connected to it. Some take less than five minutes to walk. Others are so long it takes all day to hike them. Also, there are parking areas called overlooks. From these people can enjoy the scenery without getting out of their car.

History is always present along the AT. Near Brown Mountain Creek the trail goes by land once farmed by slaves. After the Civil War (1861 – 1865), a freed man bought the land. It then became a community of former slaves who were paid for their work. This community existed until 1920. Stone cabin foundations and other reminders of those days can still be seen.

There are nearly 100 miles of the Appalachian Trail in Shenandoah National Park. Like Great Smoky Mountains National Park, Shenandoah National Park was established, in part, to help the land heal. Destructive logging and farming practices had greatly disturbed the mountains' environment.

The Civilian Conservation Corps (CCC) did much of the work in the park. The workers constructed trails, picnic areas, and buildings. President Franklin Roosevelt established the CCC during the Great Depression (1929 – 1932) to help unemployed Americans.

The pathway the CCC built is gentler than on other parts of the Appalachian Trail. There are no very steep sections. This makes it a good place for families or those just learning to hike. It is also possible to stay in two historic lodges in the park, Big Meadows Lodge and Skyland.

Originally called Stony Man Camp, Skyland was built in 1895 by George Freeman Pollock.

The park is also a good place to see lots of wildlife. Turkeys, bobcats, raccoons, and black bears have been seen by visitors, but they aren't very common. Visitors are more likely to see animals like squirrels, chipmunks, and snakes. Many people know that to see a deer they just have to visit the park.

North of Shenandoah, the trail goes into another national park. Harpers Ferry National Historic Park in West Virginia is the site of several historical events.

In 1783, Thomas Jefferson stood on a rock that the AT now goes by. He looked to where the Potomac and Shenandoah Rivers meet. He thought the scenery was spectacular. He said it was "worth a voyage across the Atlantic."

In 1794, George Washington established a federal arsenal there. An arsenal is where weapons are stored. In 1859, John Brown unsuccessfully attacked the arsenal. He wanted to steal the weapons and give them to slaves. He hoped the slaves would then use them to free themselves.

Harpers Ferry looks much like it did during the Civil War.

Appalachian Trail visitors can now watch living history demonstrations in the park. Sometimes men will be dressed in Civil War uniforms. They will march and shoot off blanks in canons and guns. Women will have old timey clothes on and act like nurses. They will patch up the make-believe wounds of the men.

The Appalachian Trail Conservancy Head-quarters and Visitor Center is also located in Harpers Ferry. Visitors can obtain information about the trail and buy maps, guides, and other books. A free work book helps children become an Appalachian Trail national park junior ranger. Those that complete the tasks can earn a badge or patch.

From Harpers Ferry, the trail crosses the Potomac River on a railroad bridge. It then enters Maryland.

Chapter 5
Mid-Atlantic States

There are only 40 miles of the AT in Maryland. So few, in fact, that some people challenge themselves to hike it all in one day.

Great blue herons use their sharp beaks to spear their food, usually fish, but also frogs, crabs, and small birds and mammals.

Southern Maryland may have the easiest section of the AT. The three miles that the trail follows on the C&O Canal towpath are flat. The pathway runs next to the Potomac River. It is a chance to see birds and animals not often found on other parts of the AT. The great blue heron is a big bird that wades in shallow water. Its wingspan is more than six feet, and it can be over four feet tall. Muskrats live in holes they dig into the towpath's banks.

Muskrats walk slowly on land,
but are very quick swimmers in the water.

The C&O Canal is almost 200 miles long. It operated from the 1830s to the 1920s. People and consumer goods were hauled in boats. These were pulled by mules from Washington, D.C. to Cumberland, Maryland.

A few miles of the towpath along the C&O Canal are now a part of the Appalachian Trail. This is the only place on the AT that bikes are allowed.

The AT then climbs South Mountain. The hiking is easy because the mountain does not have many ups and downs. It does have good views, especially in places like Weverton Cliffs, Annapolis Rocks, and High Rock.

South Mountain has seen many historic events. George Washington was 23 when he helped build a road that crosses South Mountain. This mountain was also used by slaves following the Underground Railroad to freedom. The Battle of South Mountain during the Civil War took place at Turner's Gap and Crampton Gap.

Most American know about the Washington Monument in Washington, D.C. Fewer people know about the original monument to George Washington. It was built north of Turner's Gap by citizens of Boonsboro, Maryland, in 1827. The AT goes next to it and visitors can climb steps to the top.

The border between Maryland and Pennsylvania, known as the Mason-Dixon Line, became the dividing point between slave-holding and free states. Some people think that is why the South is called "Dixie." One theory is that the name came from ten dollar bills printed in

Louisiana. That money was called a "dix," French for ten. The bills were widely used and the South became known as Dixie.

Two state parks in southern Pennsylvania have good spots to swim. There is a regular swimming pool in Caledonia State Park. The place to swim near the AT in Pine Grove Furnace State Park is more interesting. It is a lake. However, it started out as an iron ore quarry. People dug a 90-foot

The Pine Grove Iron Furnace once produced thousands of pounds of cast iron. Today only the shell of the Pine Grove Iron Works remains.

deep hole to get the ore. This was used to make iron at the nearby furnace.

The Appalachian Trail Museum is located inside an old mill house in the state park. The museum has interesting displays about the trail and hikers. The museum also has displays and special events for children. There is no charge to visit.

The Appalachian Trail Museum showcases the history of the trail and the areas surrounding it, as well as featuring a research library and hall of fame.

The state park is also famous on the AT for the "Half Gallon Club." Anyone can join by eating a half gallon of ice cream in one sitting!

The Blue Ridge Mountains come to an end as the AT drops into the Cumberland Valley. This is part of what is known as the Great Valley. It stretches from Alabama to Canada. It is a natural route that some native tribes used to travel north and south. It was also used by early settlers. It allowed them to travel southward and enabled America's expansion westward through the Cumberland Gap. Today, Interstate 81 goes through much of the valley.

The trail passes through several small towns in Pennsylvania. Two are Duncannon and Port Clinton. Both have hotels that are more than 100 years old. The hotels welcome hikers. They are places where hikers can rest and enjoy the friendship of their companions.

The Pinnacle is a popular hiking place in Pennsylvania. It is a big pile of rocks on top of a mountain. Most views from the AT are of the mountains. However, the view from The

The Pinnacle is known for its broken, jagged rocks. Many of the rocks were broken by water seeping into small cracks then freezing, enlarging the cracks until the stone broke.

Pinnacle is open farm fields alternating with bits of woodlands. It gives the landscape the look of a patchwork quilt.

It is possible to scramble down the rocks from The Pinnacle. There is a hidden cave that can be explored with a flashlight.

The farthest extent of the glaciers was Eastern Pennsylvania in the height of the ice age. They left behind many rocks, stones, and boulders when

Melting glaciers left many rocks on the ground
that would become the AT in Pennsylvania.

they melted. That is why some people complain
about hiking on the AT in Pennsylvania. However,
the worst of the rocks only lasts for a few miles.

The trail then crosses the Delaware River into
New Jersey.

The receding glaciers also created ponds
and lakes. One is Sunfish Pond on Kittatinny
Mountain. It is surrounded by thousands of
blueberry bushes. These are a delicious trailside
treat that hikers are permitted to eat. Blueberry
bushes may be only six inches tall, like those in

Virginia. The ones in New Jersey can be ten feet. Raspberries and wild strawberries are other tasty snacks along the trail when they are in season.

The trail on Kittatinny Mountain is sometimes close to houses. It may be possible to see people mowing lawns.

Volunteers spent years constructing the Pochuck Quagmire boardwalk, which was completed in 1995.

In the 1990s, volunteers built a mile-long boardwalk across Pochuck Quagmire in Vernon Valley. It allows hikers to go across without getting wet feet. Not many places on the AT are accessible to those in wheelchairs. The boardwalk is.

Soon after crossing into New York, the AT passes through the Harriman/Bear Mountain state parks area. This is where the first section of the trail was opened on October 7, 1923. The trail uses over a thousand steps to reach the top of Bear Mountain. On clear days it is possible to see the skyscrapers of New York City. That is remarkable because the city is almost 60 miles away.

The trail goes through a zoo at the bottom of the mountain. It is the one place AT visitors will be sure to see a bear. The bears' den is important

Ten Mile River is actually 15.4 miles long and extends from Amenia, New York to the Housatonic River in Connecticut.

for another reason. At about 120 feet above sea level, it's the lowest point of the entire trail.

The trail uses the half-mile long Bear Mountain Bridge to cross the Hudson River. It is a toll bridge, but hikers do not have to pay. The Hudson River is also a fjord, the only one the AT crosses. A fjord is a long narrow inlet with steep sides. Like some AT ponds, this was also created by glaciers.

As in Pennsylvania, the AT in New York has some nice places to swim. Hikers can take a short side trail to Canopus Lake in Clarence Fahnestock Memorial State Park. A few miles north, the trail crosses Ten Mile River just before entering Connecticut. There are campsites next to the river. So, it is a nice place to stay after taking a swim.

Chapter 6
New England States

The AT stays very close to New York as it goes through Connecticut. Several people important to the Appalachian Trail lived in Connecticut. Benton MacKaye, the "father of the Appalachian Trail", was born in the state. Judge Arthur Perkins of Hartford was ATC chairman in the 1920s.

After learning about the Appalachian Trail project from Judge Perkins, Ned Anderson mapped, cleared, cut, and blazed the AT from Webatuck, New York to Bear Mountain in Massachusetts.

Ned Anderson owned a farm in the Housatonic Valley. For more than 20 years he created, built, and maintained the AT in Connecticut. Yet, like many other trail volunteers, very few people know about him.

Shortly after entering Connecticut the trail goes into the Schaghticoke Indian Reservation. This is the only American Indian land the trail passes through. Some members of this tribe joined the Continental Army during the Revolutionary War. They helped America win independence from England.

Five miles of the AT is along the Housatonic River. This is one of the longest stretches that the trail goes by a river. Like those miles along the C&O Canal Towpath, this is also one of the most level portions. It is a good place for families with young children. It is easy walking and has several nice campsites.

The trail around Falls Village has a special section. The first wheelchair accessible portion built for the trail can be reached by car. So, too, can the spot next to the Great Falls of the

Housatonic River. The falls are 50 feet high. When the river has lots of water, the falls have been compared to Niagara Falls.

The name of the Housatonic River is a Mohican Indian word meaning 'place beyond the mountain.'

The AT rises above 2,000 feet in elevation on top of another mountain named Bear Mountain. This is the first time it has been this high since going through Maryland. Bear Mountain is the highest mountain that is entirely in Connecticut. Mount Greylock, 50 miles away in Massachusetts, can be seen from Bear Mountain.

The bubbling brook in Sages Ravine is a nice place
to rest before beginning the climb to Bear Rock Falls.

The 80 miles of the AT in Massachusetts may
have more chances to swim than any other part
of the trail. The swimming can begin at Bear
Rock Falls. This is just after the trail enters the
state in Sages Ravine from Connecticut. Early

mornings can be quite spectacular. The rising sun's rays are reflected by water tumbling 30 feet down the mountain.

Upper and Lower Goose Pond were created when the glaciers retreated at the end of the Ice Age. These types of connected lakes are called paternoster lakes.

Then one after the other come Guilder, Benedict, Goose, Upper Goose, Finerty, and

Gore Ponds. The Appalachian Mountain Club has a cabin at Upper Goose Pond where hikers can stay. There is also a canoe that visitors are allowed to paddle around in.

It is a long uphill hike to the top of Mount Greylock, the highest point in Massachusetts. However, there is also a road to the top if visitors want to drive up. This is one of the few places you can sleep indoors right next to the trail. There is also a restaurant that serves full meals. Bascom Lodge was built with local stone and old-growth red spruce in the 1930s. Some national park

The Veterans War Memorial Tower on Mount Greylock honors veterans from Massachusetts.

lodges look similar because their design is based on Bascom Lodge.

The AT shares its route with the Long Trail for more than 100 miles. The Long Trail in Vermont is more than 270 miles long. It goes from the Massachusetts/Vermont border in the south to the Vermont/Canada border in the north.

Several thru-hikers have claimed the sunsets from Glastenbury Mountain are some of the AT's best. The tower on top provides a 360-degree view of the mountains and surrounding woodlands.

This a good place to be in autumn. Sugar maple trees grow at lower elevations. Spruce, fir, birch, and mountain ash are at higher elevations. The leaves of some of these trees turn many different colors in the fall. It's so attractive that thousands of people, called "leaf peepers," come to Vermont to enjoy it.

There is also a tower on Stratton Mountain. The mountain is one of the places where Benton MacKaye said he first thought about creating the Appalachian Trail.

People lived in these mountains before the Long Trail and Appalachian Trail were built. It can be hard to tell this. Yet, hikers who pay close attention will see things from the past. Close to the trail may be holes that were once entrances to cellars. There are old apple trees that were

Bog bridges are also called puncheons. Volunteers may have to carry the boards many miles to build the bridges in wet places.

once a part of orchards. These trees may still have apples on them that are good to eat.

The trail in Vermont goes through many bogs that can be very muddy. Volunteers have built "bog bridges" to protect the environment near Little Rock Pond. These bridges also keep hikers' feet from getting wet and dirty, but they can be slick. Many hikers have slipped and fallen off into the mud.

The Mill River flows through narrow Clarendon Gorge. It is a popular place to swim.

It's possible to enjoy nature's own Jacuzzi in Clarendon Gorge. Mill River spins around boulders and rocks in the narrow gorge. You can get in and feel the swiftly moving, bubbly water go around you. This is such a delightful experience that families spend all day relaxing here.

The Appalachian Trail leaves the Long Trail at a place called the Maine Junction. Here the trail turns eastward toward New Hampshire and Maine.

The trail enters New Hampshire by going through Hanover, home of Dartmouth College founded in 1769. Its outing club, started in 1909, is the oldest college outdoors organization in America. The male members of the club built many trails that became a part of the AT. The college did not admit females until 1972!

The AT comes into the White Mountains on Mount Moosilauke. This is where northbound hikers of the AT go above tree line for the first time. Tree line is the point where the weather is too harsh for trees to grow. Here rock piles called cairns mark the trail.

Several trails, in addition to the AT,
enable hikers to reach the top of Mount Moosilauke.

This is a land of small alpine plants. These plants grow close to the ground to escape high winds.

Many families with children hike here. There is a group of huts available for people to stay. This means you and your family and friends can hike from one hut to another. You can spend the nights without having to carry heavy packs. No need to bring a tent, sleeping bag, or lots of extra food. The huts have bunk beds and serve dinner and breakfast. The hut staff sometimes performs skits to entertain the visitors.

Mount Washington is the highest point in the White Mountains. In 1931, a gust of wind going over the mountain was measured at 231 miles per hour. That is the fastest surface wind ever recorded in America. Yet, on top are a visitor center, weather observatory, museum, and gift shops. There is even a cafeteria.

Mount Washington is the second-highest mountain on the Appalachian Trail after Clingmans Dome.

The mountain is 6,288 feet above sea level. Hiking to the top can be hard for some people. However, the Mount Washington Auto Road lets people reach the summit by driving. The Mount Washington Cog Railway is another fun way to get there. A steam locomotive takes visitors three miles up the mountain. This allows people to enjoy the scenery while relaxing in the train cars.

Hikers of the AT entering Maine may notice that the mountains are some of the most rugged on the AT. The trail goes through Mahoosuc Notch soon after entering the state. This has been called the trail's hardest mile. Giant rocks and boulders have fallen from the mountainside into the narrow valley. The trail goes through this jumble.

Hikers crawl over and around these giant rocks. Sometimes the trail goes into small caves created by the fallen boulders. It sounds hard, but it can be fun. It is like going into a giant obstacle course in a playground or amusement park.

There is some Revolutionary War history near West Carry Pond. The AT follows the Arnold Trail

It can be a challenge trying to squeeze through narrow places between the rocks in Mahoosuc Notch.

for two miles. Colonel Benedict Arnold led an army through this area. The men were on their way to attack the British in Canada. It was very tough going through this land of muddy bogs. Their attack failed and Arnold received a leg wound. Although the attack was unsuccessful, Arnold and his men were considered heroes. A few years later, though, Arnold became a traitor to America. He sent secret messages to England and fought against his former friends.

Farther north, the AT crosses the Kennebec River. There is a person who gives free rides in a canoe to hikers. This is because it can be dangerous to wade across. The river is wide and its current can be very swift.

The section of the Appalachian Trail near its northern end is called the "Hundred Mile Wilderness." This is the longest stretch that the trail has without crossing a paved road. There are many ponds where it may be possible to see a moose. Loons, birds that dive under water to catch fish, are seen floating on tarns. A tarn is a pond created by a glacier high on a mountain.

Also high on one of the mountains is Fourth Mountain Bog. As they have in other places, volunteers have built bog bridges here. A bog may seem like just a muddy place that hinders hikers. Yet, bogs and other wetlands like them are some of earth's most fertile places. They contain many interesting plants, like the insectivorous pitcher plant. Its pitcher-shaped leaves hold some water at the bottom.

Pitcher plants can typically be found in bogs, but wild ones are being threatened by people draining the bogs, picking their flowers, and taking the plants to keep indoors.

Stiff hairs trap insects that end up falling into the pitcher. The plant's water has a chemical process that lets it "eat" the insects. This is how the plant gets nourishment to continue to grow.

Bogs are also places where there is the chance of seeing many different animals. Moose and deer live here. So, too, do a number of small creatures that like being near water. Hikers have been known to see otters, minks, weasels, and fishers.

Fishers are not named for the food they eat. Their name comes from the French word, *fichel*. This originally referred to a pelt, or the skin and fur, of another animal. Amazingly, one of the fisher's favorite foods is porcupine.

The northern end of the Appalachian Trail is on Mount Katahdin in Baxter State Park. This area is preserved because of a thoughtful governor of Maine, Percival Baxter. He started buying the land in the 1930s. He later gave it as a present for all people to enjoy.

Katahdin is an Abenaki Indian word that means "greatest mountain." This is appropriate as it is a monadnock, a mountain that stands alone. There are no other mountains around it. Thru-hikers also think it is the greatest mountain. It is where their journey of over 2,000 miles ends—or begins.

The Appalachian Trail climbs nearly 4,000 feet from the base of Mt. Katahdin to the summit.

Chapter 7
Hiking and Camping

Visiting the Appalachian Trail can be more than simply walking on it. It's possible to fish in a lake or swim in a creek. Watch a butterfly land on a pretty flower. Sleep in a trail shelter with family and friends. Cook dinner on a camp stove. Roast marshmallows over a campfire. See an animal you have never seen before. Gaze at more stars than can be seen from home. Maybe even see some shooting stars.

So, visiting the Appalachian Trail can involve many fun things. Even learning how to do it safely can be fun. Also, there is a lot of cool gear that can be taken along.

There is no need to spend a lot of money. You may already have many of these things. Others may be bought for just a few dollars. The American Hiking Society suggests the following things should be taken with you on day hikes:

- **Footwear.** There is no need for special boots to hike on the AT. Except for people with foot problems, trail shoes should be good enough. (Remember, Grandma Gatewood hiked the entire trail in tennis shoes!)

A compass may help you find your way if lost and a headlamp will help if you are out in the dark.

- **Map, compass, and guidebook.** Learn about the hike before leaving home. Look at a trail map to know where the trail is. Carry the map in your day pack. The Appalachian Trail is usually easy to follow. That is because it is marked by white paint blazes. The blazes are usually on trees. They can also be on rocks, telephone poles, and wooden posts. However, a compass should be carried. It can be fun to use it to know what direction you are hiking. Also, it will be useful if you get lost. Guidebooks for the entire trail may be bought from the ATC. They give descriptions about the trail and where to find water. The guidebooks also provide interesting facts about history and nature.

White paint blazes on trees, rocks, or posts help hikers stay on the trail.

- **Water.** Always carry extra water. The human body needs water to make its muscles and organs work properly.

- **Food.** The body also needs food, which provides energy to keep it going. Bring enough so there is some in case the hike takes longer than anticipated.

- **Rain gear and extra clothing.** Be prepared for sudden changes in the weather. Warm and sunny days can quickly become cold and rainy. It can even snow on a spring or fall day. Carry rain gear. This can be a poncho or a rain jacket and pants. Also bring an insulating layer of clothing, such as a wool sweater or a jacket. Several layers of clothing will keep you warmer than wearing just one thick layer.

- **Safety items. Flashlight and whistle.** A light of some kind should always be carried. It may get dark before the hike is finished. A flashlight is ok, but a headlamp is probably better. It lets you see, but keeps your hands free to do other things.

A headlamp may be bought for as little as one dollar in discount stores. A whistle can be heard better that just yelling. Blow on the whistle three short times if help is needed.

- **First aid kit.** A first aid kit, with bandages and other medicine, will be needed if someone gets hurt. Taking a first aid class with family or friends can be a good way to know what to do in case of an emergency.

- **A hat, sunscreen, and sunglasses.** Too much sun can cause sunburn and damage the skin. Carry sunscreen, sunglasses, and a hat. Carrying insect repellent is also a good idea.

- **Daypack.** This is what will hold all of the other items. It may not be necessary to buy a new one. The book bag used for school will most likely be good enough.

It will be necessary to bring along more things if the hike includes camping overnight:

- **Backpack.** This will be bigger than the daypack because it has to hold more things.

Shelters along the trail offer a welcome place to rest for hikers.

- **Tent.** There are more than 250 shelters along the Appalachian Trail. Anyone is allowed to sleep in them. However, most shelters will only hold about eight people. There may not be room for everyone who wants to use one. That is why a tent should be brought on an overnight hike. A tent also keeps the rain from getting hikers wet and stops mosquitoes from biting.

Deer ticks are the primary transmitters of Lyme disease, so wearing insect repellant could help prevent getting the disease.

- **Sleeping bag.** A sleeping bag keeps campers from getting cold at night.

- **Water purifier.** It will not be possible to carry all of the needed water on an overnight hike. Water found along the trail is probably not clean. It needs to be treated before drinking. Water purifiers make the water clean. There are different kinds and all are pretty nifty. Some pump water through a filter. Others let gravity pull the water through. Some are simply straws that you drink through.

- **Rope.** Human food needs to be kept away from animals. There may be a big metal box, called a bear box, close to a trail shelter. Food should be put in there overnight. It has a latch that bears and other creatures can't open. If there is no box, it will be necessary to "bear bag" your food. Put the food in a waterproof bag and tie it up in a tree. Watching someone try to bear bag can almost be like watching a comedy skit. A rock or heavy stick is tied to the end of a long rope. The person then tries to throw the rope across a limb high in a tree. Sometimes the weight comes untied. Sometimes the rope gets caught in a lower branch. It may take 10 times or more before everything works the way it should.

You have learned all of this so that you can be safe and enjoy yourself while hiking. It is also good to learn how to be kind to the environment.

The Boy Scouts and an organization called Leave No Trace developed guidelines to help you[1]:

---

1   This copyrighted information has been reprinted with permission from the Leave No Trace Center for Outdoor Ethics, www.lnt.org.

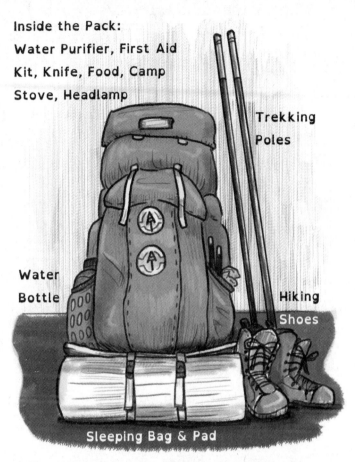

Inside the Pack:
Water Purifier, First Aid
Kit, Knife, Food, Camp
Stove, Headlamp

Trekking
Poles

Water
Bottle

Hiking
Shoes

Sleeping Bag & Pad

Thru-hikers need to be ready for anything that could happen on the trail so their packs usually contain a variety of items to keep them prepared, some of which are highlighted above.

- **Know Before You Go.** Be prepared. Bring clothes to protect from cold, heat, or rain. Use maps. Learn about the areas you visit.

- **Choose the right path.** Stay on the main trail. Many uncaring people do not follow the trail when it has switchbacks. These are spots where the trail has zigzags to make it easier to go up a mountain. Cutting switchbacks causes erosion and damages the environment. Camp at least 100 big steps from roads, trails, and water.

- **Trash Your Trash.** Pack it in. Pack it out. Carry all trash home. Act like a cat and bury poop in a small hole four to eight inches deep. Make the hole 100 big steps from any water.

- **Leave it as You Find It.** Leave plants, rocks, and historical items as you find them. Good campsites are found not made.

- **Be Careful with Fire.** Use a camp stove for cooking. Use only an existing fire ring. Keep the fire small. Only use sticks found on the ground. Be sure the fire is out and cold before leaving.

- **Respect wildlife.** Watch animals from a distance. Never approach, feed, or follow them. Human food is unhealthy for all animals. Control pets at all times.

- **Be kind to other visitors.** Make sure your fun does not bother anyone else. Listen to nature. You will see more animals if you are quiet.

Do not let all of this make you think hiking the AT is too much for you. You do not have to be in the best of shape or be a star athlete to hike the AT. It is possible to start with short hikes. Longer hikes will become easier as you become more experienced. Remember, hikers come in all shapes, sizes, and ages.

Chapter 8
Thru-Hikers

Signs and blazes help hikers keep track of the trail
and the direction they're going. Signs to Maine point
northward and signs to Georgia point southward.

Close to three million people a year hike
somewhere on the Appalachian Trail. Those
that hope to hike the entire trail in one journey
are called thru-hikers. They are a very small
percentage of those three million. Yet, they are

the most talked about because what they are attempting is so amazing.

Thru-hikers come from all over the world. Some are college students. Some are retired. Some hike alone. Some hike with friends or spouses. Some hike with their brothers, sisters, fathers, and mothers. There are also instances where hikers have met on the trail and fallen in love. They later got married.

Appalachian Trail thru-hikers can be quite old or quite young. In 2017, Dale Sanders became the oldest person to thru-hike at the age of 82. That same year, Ellie Quirin turned one year old as she accompanied her parents, Bekah and Derrick, on their thru-hike of the Appalachian Trail. In 2013, Neva Warren was only 15 years old and she hiked the entire trail alone. (Her parents met her at road crossings almost every evening.)

There have also been people with disabilities to hike the trail. Bill Irwin hiked the entire trail even though he was blind. Bob Barker hiked the trail even though he had multiple sclerosis. Scott Rogers did it even though one of his legs was amputated above the knee.

Bill Irwin's guide dog, Orient, helped
the blind hiker find his way on the trail.

It usually takes four to six months to complete a thru-hike. Some hike from south to north. Others go the opposite way. No matter which direction, thru-hikers walk many miles up and down mountains day after day. In fact, they take more than five million steps before they complete their journey.

These hikers will have to eat a lot of food to supply their bodies with the needed energy. Most people need 1,500 to 2,000 calories a day. Thru-hikers need more than 5,000. They may eat lots of nuts, candy, peanut butter and jelly, and macaroni and cheese. Yet, many still lose weight.

They can't carry enough food in their packs for the entire hike. They will buy food along the way or make what are called resupply boxes. They will put enough food for about a week in many different boxes. Then family or friends will mail the boxes to post offices along the way. The boxes will be addressed to the hiker and marked "general delivery." Anyone can get mail delivered to them this same way at any American post office.

Sometimes hikers will meet "trail angels" along the way. These are people that help hikers without asking for anything in return. A trail angel may offer hikers cold sodas on a hot day. Or give hikers a ride into town to resupply. One of the nicest things a trail angel can do is let the hikers take showers and feed them a home cooked meal.

Hikers enjoy swapping stories with each other in the evening.

Most thru-hikers take a nickname, or "trail name," while on the trek. Some name themselves, like Strider who called himself that because he took long steps. Splat named herself that because she fell down a lot. Sometimes hikers receive their name from others. Butterfly walked so lightly that hikers said she looked like she was floating. The Moonpie Kid was called that because he ate Moonpies three times a day. Wrong Way was walking south when he thought he was going north.

Thru-hikers have many different experiences together. Sometimes they are cold and wet. Sometimes they are very hot and thirsty.

They have happy times together. They may have to go through difficult times. They often share their food with each other. Thru-hikers have a tendency to look out for each other. A hiker may give another hiker a jacket to keep him or her warm. Or carry some of another hiker's gear to help lighten the load. Because they share all of these experiences, thru-hikers often become very good friends. Friends that they keep long after their hikes are over.

Chapter 9
Animals

Appalachian Trail visitors have the possibility of encountering dozens of animals. Some animals could weigh almost as much as a small car. Others may be no more than half an ounce. Some inhabit hollow trees, some live underground. Some glide gracefully in water while others zip swiftly through the air.

Many of the animals are most active at night. That may be a good incentive to camp on the trail. You might just catch a glimpse of one.

Remember that all of these creatures are wild animals. They usually leave people alone unless they feel someone is threatening them. An animal may feel threatened if a person tries to touch them or get too close. This may cause the animal to attack and harm the person. Always observe wild animals from a safe distance.

Black bears live in every state through which the AT passes. They can weigh more than 500 pounds and be six feet long.

Black Bears are the smallest bears
that can be found in the United States,
and can sprint up to 30 miles per hour.

In the early days of the national park system,
park rangers and visitors would feed the bears.
This made the animals used to getting food from
humans. These bears became a problem because
they would sometimes attack humans to get the
food. People now know that feeding wild animals
is not good.

Some people believe black bears are carnivores, that they eat just meat. However, bears are omnivorous, meaning they will consume a variety of foods. Everyone knows that bears love honey and honeycomb. However, they will also eat the bees and their larvae. Most of the meat in a bear's diet comes from small animals. This can be insects, fish, mice or chipmunks. Bears also consume roots, nuts, and berries. In addition, they have been seen climbing high into trees. There they eat small twigs and fresh leaf shoots that grow in springtime.

A thrilling thing on the AT is catching sight of a moose raising its head out of a pond. It might even be heard before being seen. Gallons upon gallons of liquid may roll off a massive set of antlers. The water drips down the muscular neck and splashes loudly into the pond. A moose's favorite food is aquatic vegetation. So, there might be a long strand of pondweed hanging from its mouth. Long legs and short necks make it difficult for them to eat in shallow water. This is why they are sometimes seen kneeling down in the water.

Moose are related to deer, but are much bigger. Sometimes bigger than a horse. A male moose may grow to be seven feet tall at the shoulders. It may then weigh almost 1,200 pounds. At one time, moose were only found in Maine. Now they are seen in New Hampshire, Vermont, and Massachusetts.

A Moose's antlers can measure more than five feet from one side to the other.

Gray wolves existed in almost all of North America when settlers first arrived from Europe. Wolves were the major predator. They kept the populations of deer, moose, and other animals in check. However, the humans feared the wolves.

They hunted and killed them. By the twentieth century there were no more wolves in the eastern United States.

Soon after, coyotes moved eastward from the western states. They began to fill the role of predator. Today, they live all along the Appalachian Trail. Although they are as big as large dogs, they are very elusive. It is a lucky person who gets to see a coyote.

Bobcats are usually only active during dusk and dawn. The word for that behavior is crepuscular. They are also very secretive and try to stay away from humans. That is why it is very rare to see a bobcat while on the Appalachian Trail. During the day they sleep in hollow trees, behind rocks, or in thick vegetation.

Bobcats are much bigger than the cats that are pets. Most pet cats weigh about 10 pounds. An average weight for a bobcat is 25 pounds. They also look different. Their ears have long hairs at the top, known as tufts. These cats received their names from their tail. Their tails are "bobbed," meaning short and stubby.

A Bobcat's fur is golden brown with streaks of black.

Bobcats live in all AT states. A larger relative, the lynx, is found on the AT only in Maine, New Hampshire, and Vermont.

Gray foxes are also crepuscular. They are related to pet dogs and have many of the same features. Their noses are long and narrow and their legs are slim. Their tails are bushier than the average domestic dog. Gray foxes are the only foxes that can climb trees. Their claws are hooked. This helps them grab onto tree trunks. Gray foxes are such good climbers that they can come down either tail or head first. They climb trees to escape predators or look for food.

Gray foxes often live in caves or hollow trees.

Gray foxes mate for life. Their children, called kits, live with the parents for only three months. Then they leave to find their own mates and territory. These foxes like to live in heavily forested areas. The habitat of a relative, the red fox, is open meadows and farm lands. The red fox has glands that produce a strong odor, much like the skunk's.

A skunk is usually peaceful by nature. If threatened, it will do a funny dance. This is a warning that it is getting ready to spray. It will stamp its feet and raise its tail. It will then do a handstand on its front paws. If this does not scare away the threat, it bends its body into a U. (Its head and rear are facing the enemy.) It lifts its tail and sprays a musky oil into the attacker's eyes.

The word skunk is from the Algonquian Indian word segahgo. It is believed that the name for the city of Chicago means "skunk place."

Another animal's name comes from the Algonquian tribe of Virginia. They called that animal an arahkun, which became raccoon in the English language.

Raccoons most often live close to water. Their paw prints are sometimes seen in the soft mud next to a stream. The hind prints almost look like a small human's foot. The front paw has a thumb. This thumb enables the raccoons to grasp their food better. They will open clams and mussels. Discarded shells show that a raccoon enjoyed a meal beside a creek.

A porcupine's body is covered by 32,000 sharp quills. It will strike with its tail when threatened. This causes the attacker to retreat.

Porcupines are most often encountered
in the AT's more northern states.

Porcupines can also cause problems for
Appalachian Trail visitors. Like all animals,
porcupines need salt. Hikers' sweaty bodies leave
salt on shelter floors and picnic tables. Some
of these structures have been destroyed when
porcupines gnaw on them for the salt. Also,
salt gets on hikers' packs, boots, and clothing
from sweat. People who forget to hang these
items at night find them chewed in the morning.
People in shelters have even had a porcupine
walking on them at night!

A Little Brown Myotis can eat half of its own body weight in insects each night. Pregnant females eat 110 percent of their body weight per night.

Bats are the only mammals that can fly. The little brown myotis bat is very common along the AT. Its wingspan is 10 inches, but it weighs less than one-half ounce. That is less than a slice of bread. The little brown myotis sleeps in barns, caves, and other dark places during the day. It feeds while flying at night. This helps control the insect population. A single little brown myotis will eat more than 2,000 mosquitoes a night.

Hundreds of bird species live in the Appalachian Mountains. Like the other animals, they can be big or small. Eagles, hawks, and herons are some of the largest. Hummingbirds are the smallest.

One of the finest bird experiences to watch is the fall hawk migration. The Appalachian Trail is one of the best places to do this. Heated air rises from the ground, creating updrafts known as thermals. Winds also strike the mountains providing more uplift. Hawks use these forces to soar upward.

Hawks have talons, or very sharp claws, on their feet that help them capture prey even while in flight.

Ospreys, American kestrels, and a few bald eagles begin flying southward in August. Thousands of other hawks, such as broad-

The American Kestrel is the United States' smallest falcon;
it weighs less than six ounces.

shouldered hawks, Coopers hawks, and red-tailed hawks, will fly over the mountains in the next few months. A thrilling thing to witness is something called a kettle. This is when hundreds of broad-winged hawks ride a thermal. They rise together creating a giant spiral in the sky.

The hawk migration comes to an end in December. Soaring over the AT that may be covered in snow are northern goshawks and golden eagles.

The great horned owl is one of the largest owls along the AT. Its wingspan is almost six feet. This owl's call is the one Hollywood movies often use. Many hikers are delighted to hear the familiar who-who-who-who sound. This usually happens just as daylight comes to an end. Sometimes one owl will call and another will answer. It can be exciting when four, five, or more call from different places.

The Great Horned Owl's ears have tufts of feathers that look like horns to some people.

Black-capped chickadees received their name from the way they look and sound. They have a black patch of feathers on the top of their head. This reminds people of a cap. The other part of their name comes from their call. It sounds like chick-a-dee-dee-dee.

Black-capped chickadees have amazing memories. They will hide seeds and other food in different places to eat later. They can remember the location of thousands of the hiding places.

Wood thrushes are forest companions for AT visitors all the way from Georgia to Maine. Their flutelike song can often be heard throughout the day. It is a pretty sound whose notes get higher near the end. This makes it easy to identify, but the bird itself is not often seen.

The wood thrush's white and brown spotted body is good camouflage. It blends in well with the dead leaves on the ground. This is where it hunts for its food. It likes to eat snails. The snail's shell provides calcium. This helps the eggs the wood thrush lays to have strong shells.

Chickadees may be found throughout North America and are the state bird of two AT states, Maine and Massachusetts.

Chapter 10
The Future of the Trail

The Appalachian Trail has been completed for many decades now. In addition, nearly every inch is protected within some kind of public land. Yet, as Myron Avery said in the mid-1900s, "...the trail, as such, will never be completed." There will always be the need to maintain the trail and cut back weeds and bushes.

Garlic mustard and kudzu can take over an entire landscape, killing all the other plants.

The spread of invasive plants such as garlic mustard and kudzu must be halted. Water bars need to be built to prevent erosion, and deteriorating shelters and trail signs need to be repaired. Fallen trees must be cleared so that visitors will have an open pathway to follow.

There will also always be the need to watch for and correct encroachments on the land. Some of these are the construction of new highways, utility towers, or nearby housing developments. Harder to define are the threats from air pollution and climate change.

The AT is also becoming a victim of its own success. Trail managers are trying to minimize the impact of rising numbers of visitors. From the 1920s to the early 1980s, only 1,000 people had hiked the entire trail. Today, the number of officially certified 2,000 milers is more than 21,000.

It is not only 2,000 milers who are on the increase. The Appalachian Trail Conservancy estimates more than three million people visit the AT annually. The challenge trail managers face is not just protecting the physical features of the trail, it is also preserving the experience of the trail's tranquil beauty.

Visitors can do their part to preserve these unique aspects. Carrying out trash, staying on the trail, and respecting wildlife help minimize impacts. These things are part of the Leave No Trace guidelines. The Appalachian Trail Conservancy is even asking hikers to register for campsites ahead of time. This is in the hope that registration will prevent overcrowding at any one particular place. Yet the Appalachian Trail is still a place to spend time in quiet thought or enjoy the company of trail friends.

The trail is still a place to appreciate this earth we live upon. It is a place to enjoy your surroundings, the shapes of the trees, and the sunlight filtering through the leaves. You can smell the forest as a summer rain washes over it and see the changing color and composition of the soil along different parts of the trail. You can listen to bird songs and watch the antics of squirrels and chipmunks. You could gaze upward to where a white cloud sails silently through the blue sky.

Possibly, this is the trail's greatest importance. Maybe more than its recreational opportunities, it is the trail's preservation of the natural world that is important. The Appalachian Trail's rare lungless salamanders may continue to exist. Birds can use a 2,000 mile unbroken forest in which to rest during their migrations. Many plants have the protection they need so that they are no longer endangered or threatened. Large mammals like bears and moose have the extensive tracts of land required to survive. These things may be the true value and legacy of the Appalachian Trail.

May all of your wanderings bring you pleasure, amazement, new discoveries, and an appreciation of the trail's many wonders.

Happy trails.

—The Habitual Hiker

Select Quotes for the Appalachian Trail

"The ultimate purpose of the Appalachian Trail? To walk. To see. And to see what you see."
—Benton MacKaye

"Those of us, who have physically worked on the Trail, know that the Trail, as such, will never be completed."
—Myron Avery

"And what is the Trail? . . . It always was a place for people. People who care for land and tend a simple footpath as if it were their garden."
—ATC *Member Handbook*

"When I started at Springer Mountain I thought I would never reach the end of the trail. Today I cried because I did."
—Laurie Messick

"Remote for detachment; narrow for chosen company; winding for leisure; lonely for contemplation. It beckons not merely north and south but upward to the body, mind and soul of man."
—Harold Allen

"[The hike was finished.] Already it seemed like a vivid dream . . . Already I knew that many times I would want to be back again—On the cloud-high hills where the whole world lies below and far away—By the wind-worn cairn where admiring eyes first welcome newborn day—To walk once more where the white clouds sail, far from the city clutter—And drink a toast to the Long High Trail in clear, cold mountain water."
—Earl Shaffer

Appalachian Trail Timeline

270 million years ago The continents that would become North America and Africa collide. This forms the Appalachian Mountains.

1859 Oil and natural gas are discovered in the Appalachian Mountains of western Pennsylvania.

1862 *Walking* is published by Henry David Thoreau, increasing the average interest in hiking.

1879 Benton MacKaye is born.

1911 Congress begins creating national forests in Eastern states.

1921 Benton MacKaye writes the magazine article proposing the Appalachian Trail.

1925 The Appalachian Trail Conference is established.

1931 Myron Avery is elected chairman of Appalachian Trail Conference.

1937 The Appalachian Trail is completed.

1948 Earl V. Shaffer becomes the Appalachian Trail's first thru-hiker.

1952 Mildred Ryder becomes the first woman to thru-hike the Appalachian Trail.

1955 Emma "Grandma" Gatewood hikes the AT for the first time.

1963 The Appalachian Regional Commission is established to battle poverty in the Appalachian region.

1968 The National Trails System Act is passed.

1971 Ed Garvey writes the book *Appalachian Hiker*. More people start hiking the trail after reading it.

World Timeline

470 million years ago The Early Cambrian Period ends.

2.8 million years ago The most recent Ice Age begins.

1861 American Civil War starts.

1865 American Civil War ends.

1879 Madison Square Garden opens.

1917 America enters World War I.

1918 World War I ends.

1929 The Great Depression begins.

1933 President Franklin D. Roosevelt starts the Civilian Conservation Corps.

1941 America enters World War II.

1945 World War II ends.

1952 Elizabeth II becomes Queen of the United Kingdom.

1955 The United States engages in an undeclared war in Vietnam.

1960 John F. Kennedy is elected president.

1963 President Kennedy is assassinated.

1969 America lands men on the moon.

1972 Video game *Pong* is released.

1975 US involvement in Vietnam ends.

1973 Warren Doyle hikes the entire Appalachian Trail the first of 17 times.

1978 Amendments to the National Trails System Act are passed.

1998 Bill Bryson publishes *A Walk in the Woods*. The book is the humorous story of his attempt to thru-hike the trail. It brings much publicity to the trail.

2005 Appalachian Trail Conference changes its name to Appalachian Trail Conservancy.

2015 The movie *A Walk in the Woods* starring Robert Redford and Nick Nolte is released in theaters.

2018 Just 1% the Appalachian Trail remains unprotected. More than 19,000 people have reported hiking the entire trail.

World Timeline (cont.)

1978 The first Global Positioning Satellite is launched into orbit by the United States.

2001 World Trade Center in New York City is attacked.

2005 Hurricane Katrina devastates the Gulf Coast of America.

2016 Mosquitoes cause an outbreak of the Zika virus.

2018 The United Nations releases a report on the urgent need for the world to address climate change.

Glossary

Alpine Plants that grow above the timberline, usually on mountaintops.

Bear bag Hikers must keep their food away from bears and other creatures at night. If there is not a bear box at the campsite, the food is put in a bag and tied up into a tree.

Bear box A bear box is a metal box, usually close to a trail shelter. Hikers put their food in it for the night. It has a latch that bears and other animals can't work open.

Blazes Blazes are two by six inch rectangles painted on trees, rocks, and other surfaces. They mark the trail so that hikers will know where it goes. The AT is marked by white paint blazes. Side trails to water sources, shelters, and parking lots are marked by blue paint blazes.

Bog A bog is land that is wet, spongy, and muddy. It usually starts out as a pond. Plants, like moss and ferns, begin to grow in it. Hundreds of years of this rotting vegetation create a thick layer of muck in the watery soil.

Cairn A cairn is a big pile of rocks. It also helps hikers know where the trail is. It is usually used above the treeline where there are no trees to put paint blazes on.

Camouflage Animals use camouflage to blend in with their surroundings so that it is hard for predators to see them. One way they do this is by having their fur or feathers look like the environment around them. An example is a wood thrush. Its feathers are different shades of brown. This makes it look like the leaves on the ground when hunting for food.

Club moss Club moss does not look like a regular moss. It has leaves that are shaped like needles. It reproduces by spores instead of seeds. Running cedar is a club moss often found beside the Appalachian Trail.

Coastal Plain Also called the Atlantic coastal plain, it is a non-mountainous part of the East Coast of the United States. It includes parts of Florida, Georgia, South Carolina, North Carolina, Virginia, Maryland, Delaware, Pennsylvania, New Jersey, New York, Rhode Island, Connecticut, Massachusetts, and Maine.

Continent Land on the Earth is divided into large land masses known as continents. Some of the continents that exist today are North America, South America, Europe, Asia, and Africa.

Continental Divide The continental divide is in the Rocky Mountains of the western United States. Rain that falls on its eastern side flows into the Atlantic Ocean. That which falls on the western side ends up in the Pacific Ocean.

Crepuscular Animals that are most active at dusk and dawn

Crustal plates Crustal plates are large land masses that drift on the earth's surface. They may slowly collide with each other over the course of millions of years.

Erosion To diminish or destroy slowly, usually by water, wind, or ice.

Fjord A fjord is a long narrow water passage with steep sides created by a glacier. The Hudson River along the Appalachian Trail in New York is a fjord.

Glacier Glaciers are very thick bodies of ice that move slowly across land. They form when snow or frozen rain falls on them year after year. Most of the time glaciers stay frozen. However, scientists believe that glaciers are now melting. This is because the Earth's temperatures are getting hotter due to global warming.

Habitat A habitat is the place where an animal makes its home. It has all the things that a particular animal needs to live. This includes places that the animal can make its nest or den. It also has the kind of food the animal likes to eat and water to drink.

Insectivorous Animals and plants that feed on insects and other small animals to get their nourishment.

Loon Loons are most often seen on the Appalachian Trail in the New England states. They are big birds that dive underwater to catch fish. They received their name because humans think they walk funny when on land.

Migration Many animals move from place to place throughout the year. This is called migration, and they do it for different reasons. Some animals migrate to find more abundant food sources. Others move to places that are warmer so they can escape cold temperatures.

Monolith A massive structure made out of a single stone, sometimes in the form of a column.

Mountains An elevated landmass larger than a hill.

Nocturnal Animals that are nocturnal are most active at night and sleep during the day. Many of the animals that live along the Appalachian Trail are nocturnal.

Omnivorous Animals that will eat both plants and animals are omnivorous. Animals that just eat plants are called herbivores. The animals that just eat meat are carnivores.

Piedmont A plateau area between the Coastal Plain and Appalachian Mountains in the United States.

Predator A predator is an animal that hunts and eats

other animals in order to live. A bear eating a mouse is a predator. Even spiders that catch flies are predators.

Quagmire Ground that sinks when stepped on, usually soft, wet, and spongy.

Tree line Tree line is the place on a mountain above which trees can't grow. This may be because the temperatures are too low or the wind is too strong for woodlands.

Underground Railroad A system of safehouses and antislavery activists that helped escaped slaves move north to freedom from the late 1700s to the mid 1800s.

Woodlands Land covered with trees and shrubs.

Bibliography

Adkins, Leonard M., *The Appalachian Trail: A Visitor's Companion*, Birmingham: Menasha Ridge Press, 2000.

Adkins, Leonard M., *Wildflowers of the Appalachian Trail*, Birmingham: Menasha Ridge Press, 2017.

Chew, Collins, *Underfoot: A Geologic Guide to the Appalachian Trail*, Harpers Ferry, WV: Appalachian Trail Conservancy, 2010.

Luxenberg, Larry, *Walking the Appalachian Trail*, Mechanicsburg, PA: Stackpole Books, 1994.

Shaffer, Earl V., *Walking with Spring*, Harpers Ferry, WV: Appalachian Trail Conservancy, 2004.

Appalachian Trail Guides (a series of 11 guidebooks available from the Appalachian Trail Conservancy).

Further Reading

Brill, David, *As Far as the Eye Can See*, Harpers Ferry, WV: Appalachian Trail Conservancy, 2010.

Hashimoto, Meika, *The Trail*, Scholastic Press, New York: 2017.

Honovich, Nancy and Julie Beer, *National Geographic Kids Get Outside Guide: All Things Adventure, Exploration, and Fun!*, Washington, D.C., National Geographic Children's Books, 2014.

Houts, Michelle, *When Grandma Gatewood Took a Hike*, Columbus: Ohio University Press, 2016.

Ross, Cindy, *A Woman's Journey*, Harpers Ferry, WV: Appalachian Trail Conservancy, 2009.

Tornio, Stacy and Ken Keffer, *Kids' Outdoor Adventure Book*, Helena, MT: Falcon Guides, 2013.

Index

Index (cont.)

Index (cont.)

Index (cont.)

Index (cont.)

About the Author

Leonard M. Adkins has hiked more than 20,000 miles exploring the backcountry areas of the U.S., Canada, Europe, and the Caribbean. Almost every hiking season finds him on some new and exciting adventure. He has hiked the full length of the Appalachian Trail five times. Leonard is the author of more than twenty books on the outdoors, nature, and travel, and his *Wildflowers of the Appalachian Trail* received the National Outdoor Book Award, ForeWord Magazine's Book of the Year Award, and a Virginia Literary Award nomination. *The Appalachian Trail: A Visitor's Companion* was honored by the Society of American Travel Writers Foundation with a Lowell Thomas Travel Journalism Award.